OPTIONS TRADING

CRASH COURSE

A Beginner's Guide To Making Profit

With Proven Strategies

DEREK W. MORGAN

TABLE OF CONTENTS

YOUR FREE GIFT

To thank you for your purchase, we're offering a free "Options Trading Checklist" exclusively for the readers of OPTIONS TRADING CRASH COURSE

Go to amazon.com and click on the preview Look inside ↓

of the kindle to access your free gift!

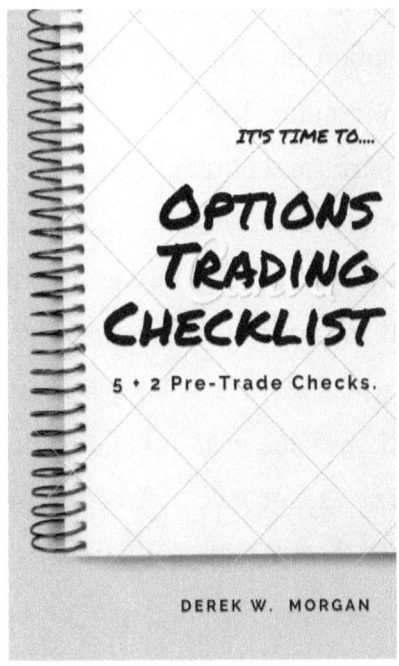

INTRODUCTION

An option is a contract that grants a buyer- the holder or owner of an option the right (and no obligation) to buy or sell the underlying asset or instrument at a specific strike price before or on a particular date, depending on the form of the option. The strike price may be determined by referring to the spot or market price of the underlying security or commodity on the day the option is withdrawn or may be fixed at a discount or a premium. The seller has the commensurate obligation to perform the transaction – to sell or buy – if the buyer (owner) exercises the option. An option that grants the owner the right to buy at a particular price is known as a call; an option that gives the right of the owner to sell at a particular price is known as a put. Both are widely traded, but the call option is discussed more frequently. The seller may offer an option to the buyer/purchaser as part of another transaction, like a share issue or as a part of an employee reward system; otherwise, the buyer will have to pay the seller a premium for that option.

A call option would usually only be exercised when the strike price is less than the market value of the underlying asset, whereas a put option will only normally be exercised when the strike price is more than the market value. When options are exercised, the cost of the asset obtained, to the buyer, is the strike price plus the premium, if any. When the expiry date of the option passes without it being exercised, the option will expire, and the buyer would lose the premium to the seller. In any case, the premium is the seller's income and, as a norm, the buyer's capital loss.

The owner of an option may sell the option to a third party in a secondary market, either in an over-the-counter transaction or in an exchange of options, depending on the option. Normally, the market price of an American-style option follows closely that the underlying stock is the difference between the stock's market price and the strike price of the option. The option's actual market price may differ based on a variety of factors, such as major option holder will need to sell the option as the expiry date approaches and lacks the financial means to exercise the option, or the buyer of an option is attempting to amass a large option holding. Ownership of an option usually does not obligate the holder to any rights related to the underlying asset, like voting rights or any underlying asset income, such as a dividend.

Trading options can seem daunting at first, but it's easily understandable if you know a few critical things. The portfolios of investors are typically built with a variety of asset classes, which may include stocks, bonds, ETFs, and sometimes even mutual funds. Options are also another asset class, and when utilized properly, they give several benefits that trading stocks and ETFs can not give on their own.

Options are part of the larger group of securities called derivatives. The price of a derivative depends on or derives from the price of something else. For example, wine is a derivative of grape, ketchup is derived from tomatoes, and a stock option is likewise derived from a stock. Options are derived from financial securities — the value of which is dependent on the price of some other asset. Examples of derivatives are puts, calls, futures, swaps, forwards, and mortgage-backed securities, among others. Options are a type of security for derivatives. The option is a derivative because its price is inherently linked to the price of something else. If you purchase an options contract, you are granted the right, but not the obligation, to purchase as well as sell the underlying asset at a fixed price on or before a certain date.

HISTORICAL USE OF OPTIONS

Contracts related to options have been used since old times. The first known option buyer was an ancient Greek mathematician and philosopher, Thales of Miletus. On a particular occasion, it was expected that the olive production of the season would be larger than normal, and during the off-season, he obtained the right to make use of a number of olive presses in the next spring. When spring arrived, and the olive harvest was larger than predicted, he exercised his options and then leased out the press at a much higher price than he had charged for his 'option.'

The book Confusion of Confusions, published in 1688, explains the trading of "opsies" on the Amsterdam Stock Exchange, outlining that "there will be limited risks for you, while the gain may surpass all your imaginations and hopes".

Puts and "refusals" (calls) became well-known trading instruments in London first in the 1690s in the reign of William and Mary. Privileges, which were options sold over the counter in America in the nineteenth century had both puts and calls for shares provided by professional dealers. Their exercise price was set at a rounded-off market price on the day or on the week that the option was purchased, and the expiry date was usually three months after purchase. They were not traded on secondary markets.

Call options have been long used to buy large pieces of land from different owners in the real estate market; e.g., a developer pays for the right to purchase a number of adjacent plots, but is not obligated to purchase these plots and may not be able to purchase all the plots in the parcel.

In the entertainment industry, film or theater producers usually purchase the right— but not the obligation — to dramatize a particular book or script.

Lines of credit grant the prospective borrower the right— but does not grant the obligation — to borrow within a specific period of time.

Traditionally, several choices, or embedded options, have been included in bond contracts. For example, several bonds can be converted into common stock at the option of the buyer or may be termed (bought back) at particular prices at the option of the issuer. Mortgage borrowers have had the option to repay the loan early for a long time, which correlates to a callable bond option.

TYPES OF OPTIONS

Options can be categorized in a few ways.

According to option rights

- Call options: these offer the holder the right — but not the obligation — to buy something at a certain price for a particular duration of time.

- Put options: these offer the holder the right — but not the obligation — to sell something at a set price for a duration of time.

According to underlying assets

- Equity Option

- Index Option

- Bond Option

- Future Option

- Commodity Option

- Currency Option

Other types of options

Another vital class of options, particularly in the

United States, are employee stock options, they are issued by a company to its employees as a means of incentive compensation. Other types of options are found in many financial contracts, such as real estate options, which are commonly used to assemble vast plots of land, and prepayment options are commonly included in mortgage loans. However, many of the valuation and principles for risk management apply across every financial options. There are two other types of options, covered and naked.

CALL AND PUT OPTIONS

T he call option offers the holder the right to purchase the stock, and the put option offers the holder the right right to sell the stock. See the call option as a down payment for a futuristic purpose.

Example of a Call Option

A prospective homeowner sees the rise of new development. That person may want the right to buy a new house in the future, but will only want to exert that right once other developments in the area have been made.

The prospective home buyer will gain from the option of buying or not. Imagine they can purchase a call option from the developer to purchase the home at probably $400,000 at whatever point in the following three years. Oh, they can — because it's a non-refundable deposit. Normally, the developer wouldn't offer such an option for free. The prospective home buyer has to contribute a down-payment to keep that right locked.

As far as an option is concerned, this cost is referred

to as the premium. It is the price of an option contract. In the home example, the deposit may be $20,000 paid by the purchaser to the developer. Let's assume two years have gone by, and new developments are underway, and zoning has been approved. The home buyer exerts the option and decides to buy the home at $400,000 because that's the contract he has bought.

The market value of the home may have been doubled to $800,000. But because the down payment is locked in a price that was pre-determined, the buyer pays $400,000. Now, in an alternative scenario, let's say zoning approval doesn't come through till year four. This is one year after this option has expired. Now the home buyer has to pay the market price since the contract is expired already. In either case, the developer will keep the initial $20,000 collected.

Example of Put Option

Think of the put option as an insurance policy. If you own your home, you're probably familiar with buying homeowner insurance. A homeowner purchases a homeowner's policy to protect his home from damage. They pay a certain amount known as the premium for a particular period of time, let's say a year. The policy has a face value and provides security to the insurance holder in the event that the home is destroyed.

What if your asset was a stock or an index investment instead of a home? Comparably, if an investor needs insurance on his / her S&P 500 index portfolio, he/she can buy put options. An investor may fear that the bear market is close and may not be willing to lose more than 10% of its long position in the S&P 500 Index. If the S&P 500 is trading currently at $2,500, he/she may buy a put option that gives the right to sell the index at $2,250, for instance, at any point during the next two years.

If the market collapses by 20% (500 points on the index) in six months, he or she would have made 250 points by being willing to sell the index at $2250 while it is trading at $2000—a total loss of just 10%. In fact, even though the market hits zero, the loss will only be 10% if this option is retained. Again, buying the option will have a cost (the premium) and, if the market does not collapse during that time, the maximum loss on the option is only the premium that was spent.

FORMS OF TRADING

Exchange-traded Options

Exchange-traded options (also known as "listed options") are a class of exchange-traded derivatives. These exchange-traded options have standardized contracts and are settled through a clearinghouse operated by the Options Clearing Corporation (OCC). As the contracts are standard, accurate pricing models are usually available. Exchange options include:

- Stock Options

- Bond options and other interest rate options

- Stock market index options or, very simply, index options

- Future Contract Options

- callable bull/bear Contract

- over-the-counter options

Over-the-counter options (OTC options), also referred

to as "dealer options," are sold between two private parties and are not included in an exchange. The terms of the OTC option are unlimited and may be specifically adapted to meet any business requirements. In general, an option writer is a well-capitalized establishment (to reduce and prevent credit risk).

Types of options commonly traded over a counter include:

- Interest rate Options

- Currency cross-rate Options

- Options on swaps.

By evading an exchange, users of OTC options can closely adjust the terms of an option contract to fit individual business requirements. In addition, OTC option transactions do not generally need to be advertised on the market and face fewer or no regulatory requirements. However, OTC counterparts have to establish credit lines with each other and comply with each other's clearing and settlement processes.

There are no secondary markets for employees' stock options, but there are few exceptions. They must be exerted by the original grantee, or they must be allowed to expire.

Exchange Trading

The most common approach to trading options is through standardized options contracts, which are identified by different futures and options exchanges. Prices and listings are monitored and can be viewed using the ticker symbol. By publishing on-going, live markets for option prices, an exchange allows independent parties to participate in price discovery and transactions. As a middleman to both sides of the transaction, the benefits of the exchange to the transaction include:

- The fulfillment of the contract is supported by an exchange credit, which usually has the highest rating (AAA)

- Counterparts remain anonymous

- Enforcing of market laws to guarantee transparency and fairness

- Maintenance of organized markets, especially under rapid trading conditions.

Basic trade (American style)

These trades are defined from a speculator's point of view. These can also be used in hedging if they are paired with other positions. Currently, an option contract in US markets symbolizes 100 shares of the underlying security.

Long call

A trader who anticipates an increase in the price of the stock may purchase a call option to buy the stock at a fixed price ('the strike price') at a later date instead of purchase the stock outright. The cash outlay of the option is the premium. The trader would have no obligation to purchase the stock but is only entitled to do so on or before the expiry date. The risk of loss would be restricted to the premium paid, as opposed to the possible loss if the stock had been purchased outright. The holder of the American-style call option may sell the option holding at any point in time until the expiry date and would think of doing so if the spot price of the stock is greater than the exercise price, in particular, if the holder expects the option price to fall. By selling the option early in that circumstance, the trader can realize an instant profit. Alternatively, the trader may exercise the option — for

instance, if there is no secondary market for options —
and then sell the stock and make a profit. A trader would
realize a profit if the selling price of the shares increased
more than the premium. For instance, if the exercise price
is 100 and the premium paid is 10, if the spot price of 100
increases to just 110, the transaction is break-even; a rise
in the stock price above 110 generates a profit.

If at expiration the stock price is lower than the
exercise price, the holder of the options at that time will
allow the call contract to expire and will only forfeit the
premium (or the price paid on the transfer).

Long put

A trader who anticipates that the price of the stock will
fall may purchase a put option to sell the stock at a set
price ('the strike price') at a later date. The trader is not
obligated to sell the stock but has the right to do so on or
before the expiry date. If at expiration, the stock price is
less than the exercise price by more than the premium
paid, that will be a profit. If at expiration, the stock price
exceeds the exercise price, he will allow the contract to
expire and only lose the premium paid. The premium as
well plays a key role in the transaction, as it boosts the

18

break-even point. For instance, if the exercise price is 100, and the premium paid is 10, then the spot price from 100 to 90 is unprofitable. If the spot price is less than 90, he will make a profit.

It is necessary to note that an individual who exercises a put option does not actually need to own the underlying asset. Specifically, it is not necessary to own the underlying stock in order to sell it. The reason is that the underlying stock can be sold short.

Short call

A trader who expects the stock price to fall may sell the stock short or, instead, sell or "write" a call. The trader selling the call has a commitment to sell the stock to the call buyer at a set price ('the strike price'). If, when the option is exercised, the seller does not own the stock, he is obliged to buy the stock from the market at the market price at that time. If the stock price declines, the call seller/call writer will earn a profit on the amount of the premium. If the price of the stock increases over the strike price by greater than the amount of the premium, the seller will make a loss, and the potential loss will be unlimited.

Option Styles

Options are categorized into a variety of styles. These are the most common:

• American option – this is an option that may be exercised on or before it expires on any trading day.

• European option – this is an option that can only be exercised when it expires.

They are often characterized as vanilla options. Other styles include:

• Bermudan option – this is an option that can only be exercised at specific dates on or before the expiration date.

• Asian option – this is an option whose payoff is calculated by the underlying average price over a pre-determined period of time.

• Barrier option – this is an option with the general feature that the underlying security price must exceed a particular level or "barrier" before it can be exercised.

• Binary option – this is an all-or-nothing option. It pays the complete amount if the underlying security satisfies the given expiration condition else it expires.

• Exotic option – any of the wide range of options that could include complex financial structures.

DIFFERENCE BETWEEN OPTIONS AND STOCKS

What is a stock?

A stock (also called equity) is a security that signifies the ownership of a part of a corporation. This entitles the stock owner to a percentage of the assets and profits of the corporation equal to how much of the stock they own. Units of stock are referred to as "shares."

Stocks are purchased and sold mainly on the stock exchanges, but they can also be traded privately and are the cornerstone of many portfolios of individual investors. These transactions must comply with government regulations that are established to protect investors from fraudulent activities. Historically, these stocks have outpaced several other investments over the long term. These investments can be bought from most online stock brokers.

Major differences between stock and options

Both Stock and Options are common choices on the market, but they differ in several ways.

• Stocks are generally regarded as business investments that continue to do well in the long run and are thus invested for the creation of wealth, such as real estate, gold, etc. Options are used primarily as instruments for trading used to trade the movements of stock prices.

• Stocks come with ownership benefits such as stock bonuses, dividends, voting rights. Options come with no special benefits for the holder of an option.

• Stocks used as investment instruments are used with a long term period of more than 6 to 10 years. Meanwhile, options are more short-term options that range from a few weeks to months for portfolio hedges.

• Stocks are utilized by individuals, pension fund managers, mutual fund managers, brokers, and portfolio managers. Options are limited to use by traders and managers of a portfolio (as a hedging tool)

• Options are simply rights obtained by paying the

premium to buy or sell a stock at a particular price where the buyer of the option is not obliged to do the same, which is why its downside is minimal. Stock buyers are obliged to bear the full drawbacks of the stock.

WHY CHOOSE OPTIONS RATHER THAN STOCKS?

Trading options is somewhat different from trading stocks since options have different characteristics from stocks. It is essential for investors to take out time to comprehend the terms and concepts involved in options before trading them. Options are financial derivatives, which means that they obtain their value from the underlying stock or security. Options grant the buyer the right, not the obligation, to buy the underlying stock, as well as sell it at a pre-determined price.

Trading stocks can be likened to gambling in a casino: you bet against the house, and if all the customers have an amazing run of luck, they might all win.

Trading options is much like betting on horses on the racetrack: each individual bets against all other people there. The track merely takes a slight cut to provide the facilities. Trading options, such as betting on a horse race, is a zero-sum game. The gain of the option buyer is the loss of the option seller and vice versa.

One major difference between stocks and options is that the stock gives you a small share of ownership in a company, while the options are simply contracts that grants you the right to buy and also sell the stock at a particular price by a given date.

It is necessary to bear in mind that there are always two sides to every option transaction: the buyer and the seller. In other words, there's always someone else selling it for every option that is purchased.

Low Entry Cost

This is actually simple arithmetic: options are cheaper to purchase than stocks from which they get their value. If a stock is priced at $50 per share, it would cost $5,000 to buy 100 shares. On the other hand, an at-the-money call option that allows you to control 100 shares could cost you $200. If you purchased 100 shares or a call option contract, you have a long 100 shares of the stock. However, when you purchase the option rather than the stock, you reduce your entry cost significantly. As a result, not only do you risk less, but you also leave more investment capital open for other opportunities.

Leverage

Generally, by comparison, call option owners do not receive dividends or any other cash allocations. But they do benefit from leverage if their market view is correct.

When an investor purchases a call option and the underlying equity increases above the exercise price (or falls below the exercise price in the case of a put option buyer), the investor will benefit from the leverage.

The lower entry cost is a major sign of leverage as an options-related benefit. Since the option is cheaper to purchase than the same amount of stock, there is a greater opportunity for incredible percentage returns on your investment. Again, this is just a straightforward number — it's just a lot simpler to double your money on an investment of $200 than an investment of $5000.

Limited risk

Buying calls or puts enables investors to locate themselves for an expected market change by paying the option premium to the option seller. The most they will lose is the premium, which could possibly be all of their investment funds. The experience of option buyers differs from the situation of puts and call sellers. Once, option sellers would have their own specific view of the market. In a case of the put seller, she hopes that prices will rise in such a way that she can hold the premium at expiration and probably sell another put to create more income or purchase the underlying one in a case of a put that's been exercised.

In the case of a call seller, he hopes that the rates will stay flat below the call strike price. If the market doesn't move as expected, the option will be exercised, and the call seller will be obligated to sell the underlying in the case of an exercised call. This will involve a considerable cash outlay, only partially offset by the premium received.

The uninitiated could incorrectly believe that options are naturally risky. Myths abound as to the potential problems of trading options, and the very mention of the term "derivatives" is just enough to give some investors poor flashbacks to the 2008 financial crisis. However, if you buy puts and calls, you actually risk less capital than if you directly trade the stock. In the standard option-buying strategy, the total potential loss is restricted to the original amount you paid to purchase the contract(s). Sure, there is a probability that you will lose 100% of your investment if the trade is turned against you. Nonetheless, to return to the above-mentioned hypothetical——if the stock drops to zero, you'd probably prefer a 100% loss on your $200 call option than a 100% loss on your $5,000 share value.

Flexibility:

Although stocks are paving the way for long and short-term investments, options include a variety of strategic investment alternatives. Traders can purchase calls to simulate stock ownership, purchase puts to simulate short sale, or combine calls and puts to reap the benefits from upward, downward, to horizontal stock movements, through options. Options let you decide how and when to make a profit from your investment.

For the larger part, stock traders have two alternatives: long/bullish or short/bearish. On the other hand, options players have a broad wide range of strategies at their fingertips. Calls and puts can be used in a number of ways to reap the benefits of some kind of price action: bullish, bearish, sideways, and everything in between. Seasoned speculators can disregard price action in its entirety and instead use options to benefit from dividend payments or changes in implicit volatility. In addition, options can be sold to create income from existing stock positions or to set the cost of entry on a planned purchase of shares. Rather than being confined to a full black-and-white stock trading palette, you can use options to fine-tune your strategy to any market setting.

RISKS ASSOCIATED WITH OPTIONS AND HOW TO HANDLE THEM

Any investment carries a particular amount of risk. Investing options carry a higher risk, so make sure you weigh the pros and cons of the strategies you may be considering before you start trading actively.

Without going into the Greek discussion (e.g., delta, theta, gamma), the risks listed below are among the most popular in investing options. Once you create an Options Trading Account, you will receive a full guide to options trading risks from your broker.

Time Is Not exactly On Your Side.

All options expire — most of them at zero value. Unlike investing stocks, time isn't your buddy when holding long options. As the option draws closer to expiration, the premium deteriorates.

This deterioration is very fast and speeds up in the final

days before the expiration date. For an options investor, you should just spend a dollar amount that you're fine losing because you might lose it all.

There are three things to do to place time on your side:

• Purchase options at the money (or near money).

• Trade options with expiry dates that comfortably cover the investment opportunity.

• Purchase options at a stage where you believe that volatility is underpriced and sell options at that stage when you believe that volatility is overpriced.

Prices can move quickly.

As options are high leverage investments, prices move very quickly. Unlike stocks, Options prices will move by significant amounts within minutes or even seconds rather than hours or days.

Depending on factors such as the time to expire, and the connection of the stock price to the option's strike price, little movements in the stock can translate into large movements in the underlying options. But how will an options investor make money when he or she has been watching options pricing in real-time the whole day?

You should invest in opportunities where you know that the profit potential is so robust that the price of the second would not be the key to making money. In other words, go for huge profit opportunities, and there'll be a lot of incentive even if you're not accurate in your selling.

In fact, do whatever you can to organize the options purchase with the correct strike prices and the expiration months so that most of this risk is minimized. Depending on your personal tolerance for risk, you may also consider closing your option trades with sufficient time before expiry to ensure that the time value does not deteriorate too drastically.

Losses On Naked Short Positions can be significant

Like shortening stocks, shortening options naked (i.e., selling options without hedging positions through other options or stock holdings) could lead to significant and even unlimited losses.

Naked short in options means that you're selling a put or a call alone, without protecting it with cash or any other stock or option position. You might be wondering how else you would be able to sell a put or a call. Several investors choose to sell puts or calls in conjunction with stock or other options. It removes the potentially infinite possibility of a "naked" call or put being sold. The covered call section is an example of this type of technique.

While many would use the word "short" to describe selling options to open, it's not quite the same concept as stock shorting. When you short a stock, you're selling stock that's been borrowed. You have to restore the stock to its owner at some point in the future (usually through your broker). With options, you're not borrowing any protection. You simply accept the obligations associated with the sale of options in exchange for the payment of the premium.

What makes shortening options naked (also known as selling volatility) so enticing is the prospect of a steady stream of profits. Most of the professional investment community has had profits from selling options, as the underlying stocks have become less volatile than their premium options indicated.

For instance, if near-the-money 12-strike May puts

was sold in Toyota Motor and collected 58 cents, the premium would be retained if the stock stayed above $12 per share until May expires. The short put reaches its full potential profit if Toyota goes higher, remains on, or even falls a bit to the 12 strikes. Most of the time, stocks don't move as much as investors would anticipate.

There's a significant distinction between selling to open a call naked and a naked put. When you're selling a naked call, your theoretical risk is endless. You're on the hook for the distinction between the strike price and the amount the stock progresses above that price. Since there is no limitation to how much a stock can trade, the potential loss is limitless.

Nevertheless, when you sell to open a put naked, the total loss is the distinction between the strike price and zero. The risk for a naked put that's been sold is the same downside risk as to own the underlying stock at the strike price. In other words, stocks can not trade below $0, so your potential loss is enclosed, although for some high-priced stocks, dropping to $0 may seem almost limitless!

Selling puts naked can be a perfect way to get long exposure to stock at a better price. You may be looking at a stock, but the stock just seems too expensive. Instead of chasing the stock price, you can just sell a put, collect the premium for selling it, and become long the stock at your strike price if the shares move to that strike price.

For instance, you may have wanted to own Microsoft at one of its market rallies, but paying above $30 for a share seemed expensive. Instead of paying that much, you might sell the Microsoft puts for October 30 for $1.50. You obtain this premium today, and the effective cost for Microsoft is $28.50, i.e., $30 strike price minus $1.50 collected if you are obliged to purchase the stock (or "put to" the stock).

If you are interested in a put-selling strategy, it is recommended to start a little. Get a sense of what types of results are possible on a personal level. Be sure you're investing just the amount of money you're willing to lose.

When you enter options trading with wide eyes and realistic expectations, you'll be effective at handling your trades and, in turn, your risks. Again, just put 3 % to 5% of your funds for trading in each transaction. That way, if the trade goes differently than expected, you won't lose your shirt and find it difficult to recover from the loss.

Another great way to get acquainted with trading options before you use real money is to do paper trading, which means you're tracking options trades "on paper" from beginning to end without investing any money. This will enable you to develop some confidence and skills without actually risking your money until you have a deeper knowledge of how trading options work. One easy way to "paper trade" is through a virtual account with your online broker.

Options open sellers to unlimited/augmented losses. In contrast to the option buyer (or holder), the option seller (writer) may incur losses much higher than the contract price. Remember, when an investor writes a call or a put, he or she is obliged to purchase or sell shares at a particular price within the timeframe of the contract, even if the price is not favorable (and there is no limit on how high the stock price may rise).

The time for the investment thesis to bear out is limited. The exact nature of the options is short-term. Options investors seek to leverage on a near-term price movement that must take place within few days, , or even months for the trade/contract to be paid off. This requires making two correct assumptions: choosing the right time to purchase an options contract, and choosing exactly when to exercise, sell, or leave before the option expires. Investors of long-term stock do not have a deadline. They have sufficient time — years, sometimes decades — to allow their investment theses to occur.

Potential traders must comply with other specifications. You must apply for approval via your broker before you can begin trading options. After answering a number of questions about your financial means, experience in investing, and understanding the inherent risks of trading options, the broker will allocate you a trading level that defines what kind of options trade you are allowed to place. Any investor who trades options must have a minimal amount of $2,000 in their brokerage account, which is a requirement of the industry and an opportunity cost worthy of consideration.

Options investors can incur extra costs that affect their profit and loss performance. Many strategies in options trading (such as selling call options on securities that you don't currently own) will require investors to establish a margin account — which is simply a line of credit that acts as collateral in the event that a trade moves against an investor. Each brokerage firm has various minimum standards for opening a margin account and will frame the amount and rate of interest on the amount of cash and securities in the account. Margin loan interest rates usually range from low single digits to low double digits.

If the investor is not able to make good on loan (or if the balance of the brokerage account falls below a certain amount, as may be the case due to regular market fluctuations), the lender may issue a margin call and liquidate the investor's account if he /she doesn't add more funds or stocks to it.

HOW TO START OPTIONS
TRADING

A lthough it seems complex and can include a wide range of strategic approaches, it's relatively easy to start trading options.

You need a broker, and you will need to compare fees and account minimums so that you can choose one that is affordable and meets your investment style.

From there, it's time to develop your strategy for trading options. Like most investment options, trading strategies is dependent on your personal goals and tolerance for risk and can range from simple to complex.

STEP BY STEP GUIDE TO TRADING OPTIONS

STEP 1: Create a brokerage account.

If you're interested in trading options, you'll need to open a brokerage to access your transactions — this can be done online or through a standard broker account. Be sure you fully grasp what's involved in creating a brokerage account before you do that.

Compare the options trading commissions between different brokerages. Some firms do not even offer commissions on trading options.

Carry out some research online and read the reviews of brokerage firms that are on your shortlist. Gain knowledge from the mistakes of other people so you won't have to repeat them.

Observe for scam trading platforms and sites. Always thoroughly research the platform before you deposit any money. Avoid any platform with negative reviews or possible fraud reported.

A cash account will only permit the purchase of options to create a position. If you desire to sell an option to set up an account without the underlying asset, you will need a margin account.

If you want to trade online, make sure that your online brokerage accepts secure forms of payment, like a secure credit card payment gateway or a third party payment service such as PayPal, Payoneer, skrill, bitcoin, etc.

Step 2: Get approval to trade options.

You will need approval from your brokerage before you start buying and selling options. Brokerage firms handling an account set limits on the basis of experience and money in the account, and every firm has its own criteria to ensure that the customer knows what they are doing. You can't write a covered call without an options account. Brokerage firms want to make sure that customers have a full understanding of the risks before trading.

Covered call writing means selling the right to purchase your stock at a strike price during the duration of the option. The buyer has the right to do so, not the seller. The stock must be in the brokerage account and can not be sold or exchanged while the call is pending.

STEP 3: Understanding technical analysis.

Options are typically short-term investments, so in the near future, you will be searching for price movements of the optioned security to make a healthy return. In order to accurately forecast these price fluctuations, you would need to grasp the fundamentals of the technical analysis.

Learn about the level of support and resistance. These are points where the stock hardly ever decreases below (support) or increases above (resistance). Support is the level at which significant security purchases have historically occurred. Resistance is the price level, where significant security sales have occurred in the past.

Understand the significance of the volume. If a stock changes towards a specific direction with a lot of volume behind it, it typically means a strong trend and can be a money-making opportunity.

Understand the patterns of the chart. History usually repeats itself, even in the case of stock prices. There are common trends that you can look for in stock price fluctuations that can show where the price is going.

Learn more about moving averages. It is the same case when the stock price is above or below the common moving average of the previous prices. A 30-day moving average is perceived to be more accurate than a 10-day moving average.

STEP 4: Start with "paper trading."

Resist every temptation to risk hard-earned money with a technique you've just learned.

Instead, go for paper trading or practice. Make use of a spreadsheet or a practice trading software to enter "pretend" trades. Then review your returns for at least a few months. If you make a decent return, work your way to real trading slowly.

Paper trading is different from real trading, as there is no mental pressure or commissions involved. It's a good idea to learn mechanics, but it's not a predictor of actual results. Real options trading is a very high risk, which can result in substantial losses for the investor. You can only trade with money that you can afford to lose.

STEP 5: Use the limit orders.

Avoid having to pay market prices for options, as the execution price can be higher than expected. Instead, state your price with limit orders and maximize your return.

STEP 6: Reassess your strategy on a regular basis.

Determine if there is anything that can be done to enhance your return. Learn from your mistakes, but repeat your effective strategies as well. And maintain a focused strategy; traders concentrate on a few positions, not on diversification. You should have not more than 10% of your investment portfolio in options.

STEP 7: You can join a forum of traders of like minds online.

If you're experimenting with advanced trading options strategies, you'll discover that a vital source of information (and help, after a few tough losses) is an online trading platform. Locate a forum to enable you to learn from the successes and, also, the failures of others.

STEP 8: Think of other strategies for trading options.

After you have made some successful trades, you can get cleared for more advanced options trading strategies.

However, start trading on paper as well. This will make it much simpler for you to carry them out in real trading.

One such strategy is the 'straddle,' which includes trading on both sides of the market, purchasing a put and a call option with the same strike price and date of maturation, so that you restrict your exposure. This strategy is most successful when the market moves up and down rather than in a single direction. There is also a risk that only one side will be exercisable.

A related strategy is the "strip." The strip is like a straddle but is actually a "bearish" strategy with twice the earning power of a downward price movement. It is comparable to the straddle in its implementation, but with twice as many options purchased on the downside (put options).

STEP 9: Know more about the Greeks.

Once you've perfected simple options trading and choose to move on to more advanced options trading, you will have to learn about the "Greeks. "These are measures that traders use to maximize their returns.

Delta- this is the amount by which an option price

changes according to the price movements of the underlying asset. The .5 delta option will have a movement of half that of the underlying asset. If the stock moves by $1.00, the option price will be $0.50.

Gamma- The rate the delta is going to change on the basis of a $1 change in stock price.

Theta- this is the "time decay" of the price of the option. It checks how much the price decreases as the option draws closer to expiration.

Vega- this is the amount of the option price changes on the basis of the volatility of the underlying asset.

KEY TERMS IN OPTIONS TRADING

STRIKE/EXERCISE PRICE

The strike price is the price for each share at which the holder may buy (call options) or sell (put options) the underlying stock.

EXERCISE

Exercise is the mechanism by which the option purchaser (holder) incites the terms of an option contract. In the event of exercising, calls buy the underlying stock and put owners sell the underlying stock under the conditions set out in the option contract. All option contracts that are in-the-money (i.e., at least one cent of intrinsic value) at expiration will be exercised automatically.

EXPIRATION DATE

The expiration date is the last day upon which option may be exercised. The monthly stock options stop trading on the third Friday of every month and expire on the next day. The weekly options stop trading on Friday of that week.

HEDGING:

Hedging is a conservative approach used to minimize investment risk by enforcing a transaction that compensates for an existing position.

COVERED CALL

A call option that is written or sold against an already existing stock position is a covered call. The call is covered by the underlying stock that could be delivered if the call option is exercised.

INTRINSIC VALUE

An option's intrinsic value is the amount of profit that can potentially be gained if the option is exercised at that time, and the stock is either bought (for a call) or sold (for a put) at the current market price. If an option possesses a positive intrinsic value, it is "in-the-money" (ITM), and if it has an intrinsic negative value, it is "out-of-the-money" (OTM). For example, ABC January 25 Call would have an intrinsic value of $1.50 if the stock traded at $26.50, irrespective of its market price at that time.

TIME VALUE

This is the amount by which the market price of an option surpasses its intrinsic value. In the above case with ABC January 25 Call priced at $3.00 while ABC is trading at $26.50, the value is $1.50, and the residual $1.50 is time value. If an option is out-of-the-money (i.e., it does not have intrinsic value), then the whole market price is called time value.

PREMIUM

Premium is the price of an option. Prices are quoted per share, but the premium is usually the total money value of the contract (i.e., the price per share X 100 shares = total premium).

TIME DECAY

Since options have a date of expiration, all options are wasting assets whose time value is reduced to zero by expiration. This reduction is referred to as time decay. Time value differs with the square root of time, such that the rate of time decay increases as the option reaches its expiration date.

LONG:

To be "long" an option means simply to have bought it in the opening transaction and, therefore, to own or hold it.

SHORT

To be short an option implies to have sold an option in the opening transaction. (The short position is taken as a negative on the statement and must be bought later to close it.)

LEAPS (LONG-TERM EQUITY ANTICIPATION SECURITY)

T hese are long-term options that have expiration dates of up to three years, commonly expiring in January.

EX-DIVIDEND DATE/EX-DATE

This is the day before the date on which the investor had to buy the stock in order to collect the dividend. On the ex-dividend date, the closing price of the previous day is decreased by the amount of the dividend because the purchaser to collect the dividend payment on the ex-dividend date will not receive it. This date is sometimes simply known as an ex-date and may apply to several other situations (e.g., splits, distributions). If you buy a stock on the ex-date for a stock or a distribution, you aren't entitled to the split stock or distribution. Nevertheless, the opening price of the stock would have been decreased by a significant amount, as at the ex-dividend date. Every week, financial publications often include the upcoming ex-date of a stock as part of their stock tables.

EXCHANGE TRADED FUNDS (ETFs)

These are index funds or trusts enlisted on an exchange and traded in a manner similar to that of single equity. The first ETF came into being in 1993 with AMEX 's concept of a tradable stock basket — Standard and Poor's Depositary Receipt (SPDR). The number of ETFs that trade options grow continuously and diversify today. Investors can purchase or sell shares in the collective performance of the entire stock portfolio (or bond portfolio) as a single security. Exchange-traded funds help investors to enjoy some of the more desirable features of stock trading, like the ease of equity style and liquidity, in a more conventional index investing setting.

FENCE

A protection strategy where a written call and a long put are attached to a previously owned long stock position, it is also referred to as a collar. Options could have the same or different strike prices. The months of expiration may or may not be the same. For instance, if the investor had previously purchased ABC Corporation at $46 and increased to $62, the investor would be able to create a collar involving the buying of a put for May 60 and the writing of a call for May 65 as a means of preserving some of the unrealized profits in the stock position of ABC Corporation. An investor may also use the reverse, i.e., a long call combined with a written put if he has initially established a short stock position in ABC Corporation.

HOLDER:

A holder is a person who has made an opening purchase transaction, put or call and holds that position in a brokerage account.

MARK-TO-MARKET

This implies an accounting mechanism whereby the price of securities that are held in an account is valued on a daily basis to represent the closing price or market quotes. As a result, the equity in the account is updated on a daily basis to represent current security prices appropriately.

MARKET ORDER

This is a trading order issued to a broker to

immediately purchase or sell a stock or an option at the best price available.

OPTION PERIOD

The time from which the purchaser or the writer of an option creates an option contract to the date of expiration, referred to sometimes as an option 's lifetime.

OTC OPTION

The over-the-counter option is traded on the over-the-counter market. OTC options aren't listed on an exchange of options and do not have standard terms. These are to be differentiated from the exchange-listed and traded equity options, which are standard.

PHYSICAL DELIVERY OPTION

This is an option whose underlying entity is a physical commodity or good, such as common stock or a foreign currency. When the owner exercises that option, the physical goods or commodities are delivered from one brokerage or trading account to the other.

OPTION WRITER

An option contract seller who is obliged to comply

with the terms of delivery if the option owner exercises his/her right. The seller has made an opening sale transaction and has not yet closed the position.

IN-THE-MONEY / IN-THE-MONEY OPTION

The term used to define an option with an intrinsic value. In the case of standard options, a call option is said to be in-the-money if the stock price is above the strike price. The put option is in-the-money if the price of the stock is less than the strike price.

OUT-OF-THE-MONEY / OUT-OF-THE-MONEY OPTION

This is a term used to describe an option that does not have an intrinsic value. The premium for the option is completely time value. In the case of standard contracts, the call option is out-of-the-money if the price of the stock is below its strike price. The put option is out-of-the-money when the stock price is higher than its strike price.

NAKED OR UNCOVERED OPTION

A short option position that is not completely protected if assignment notification is received. A short call position is said to be uncovered when the writer doesn't have a long stock or deeper in-the-money long call position. A short put is uncovered when the writer does not have a short stock or a long deeper in-the-money position.

UNDERLYING ASSETS

What's an underlying asset

The underlying asset is a financial asset on which the price of the derivative is based. Options are examples of a derivative. A derivative is a financial tool that has a price that is based on a different asset.

Underlying assets give value to derivatives. For instance, the stock ABC option gives the holder right to buy or sell ABC at the strike price up till the expiration date. The stock of XYZ is the underlying asset for the option.

The underlying asset may be used to identify an item within the agreement that adds value to the contract. The underlying asset gives support to the security involved in the agreement, which the parties involved make an agreement to exchange as a part of the derivative contract.

Derivative Contracts

An option price or futures contract is derived from the

price of the underlying asset. In an option contract, the writer has to either purchase or sell the underlying asset to the purchaser on the specified date at an agreed price. The purchaser is not obliged to buy the underlying asset, but they may exercise their right if they want to do so. If the option is about expiring and the underlying asset has not progressed favorably enough to render exercising of the option worthwhile, the purchaser may allow it to expire and lose the amount paid for the option.

Futures is the obligation to the buyer and the seller. The seller of the future decides to supply the underlying asset at the expiration, and the buyer agrees to purchase the underlying asset at the expiration. The price they earn and pay is the price at which they have entered into a futures contract. Many futures traders close their positions before the expiration date, as retail traders and hedge funds have less need to take physical possession of oil barrels, for instance. But they can purchase or sell a contract at a particular price, and if it changes favorably, they can get out of the trade and earn a profit that way. Futures is a derivative since, for example, the price of an oil futures contract is dependent on the movement of oil prices.

Example of underlying assets

The underlying asset is the stock, in the case of stock options. For instance, with an option to purchase 100 shares of Company A at $100, the underlying asset is the stock of Company A. The underlying asset determines the value of the option up to its expiration date. The underlying asset's value could change, influencing the value of the option before the contract expires. At any given time, the value of the underlying asset helps traders know whether or not the option is worth exercising.

A currency or stock index, such as the S&P 500, may also be the underlying asset. In the case of the stock indexes, the underlying asset consists of common stocks within the stock market index.

STRIKE PRICE

The strike price (also referred to as the exercise price) is simply the fixed price at which an option contract may be exercised.

When negotiating a trade, the strike price is vital to the option buyer as it dictates the price at which they will purchase or sell the stock in the future (or, if they choose not to participate, how much profit/loss will result from the trade). For the seller, the strike price is significant when entering the market as it has a direct effect on how much credit they earn from selling the option.

Once a trade has been established, the direction of the underlying moves relating to the strike price dictates the profitability of the trade.

Strike prices are typical of equal distance from one another and are normally $.50, $1, $5, or $10 wide (although there are some basics where this is not the case, they are unusual).

CALL OPTIONS STRIKE PRICES

An agreement where the purchaser has the right to purchase 100 shares of the stock from the seller before the option expires at a fixed price, is the call option. What exactly is the price?

The strike price

The buyer of the call may choose to (but is never obliged to) exercise the option at the strike price at any particular time, and the seller must sell 100 shares to the buyer if he, i.e., the buyer decides to exercise the option contract.

If the call option becomes expired out of the money (i.e., the strike price is greater than the stock price), the seller will be able to keep the credit received, and the buyer will lose the debit that was paid for the trade.

If the call option becomes expired in the money (i.e., the strike price is less than the market price), the call buyer may exercise the option to retain shares or sell the option back for profit. If the purchaser exercises the option, the seller has to sell 100 shares of the stock at the price of the strike.

Let's examine this some more by looking at the example of the call option strike price.

EXAMPLE OF CALL OPTION STRIKE PRICE
Let's say Mr. A is buying a call in AAPL from Mr. B because Mr. A is expecting the price to increase in the next month or thereabout.

Since Mr. B is selling the call, it's alright to assume that Mr. B thinks the AAPL price is going to fall.

Currently, AAPL is trading at $145.42. The call option strike price Mr. A is looking to purchase is (b) $150 (Mr. A believes that the price of AAPL will be higher than the strike price before it expires). If Mr. B decides to sell the call option to Mr. A at the agreed strike price of $150, Mr. B will get a credit of (c) $220.

Mr. A then pays Mr. B a debit of (c) $220 for the opportunity to purchase 100 shares of the stock from him at the negotiated strike price before the option expires.

As a call buyer, Mr. A is looking for an option that will

expire in the money (i.e., the stock price is above the strike price) so that he can exercise that option.

As the call seller, Mr. B is looking for the stock price to stay out of the money (the stock price is less than the strike price).

PUT OPTIONS STRIKE PRICE

The put option is the reverse of a call option. The purchaser has the right to sell 100 shares of the stock at the given strike price before the expiration date for the put option.

The put buyer has the right (but is not obliged) to exercise the option at the strike price at any time before the expiration date, and the seller has to purchase 100 shares of the stock if the purchaser decides to exercise the option.

When the put expires out of the money (the strike price is less than the stock price), the seller will hold on to the credit they have earned, and the buyer may lose the debit paid to place the trade.

When the put option expires in the money (i.e., the strike price is higher than the stock price), the buyer of the put can exercise the option for 100 shares of the stock or sell it back for profit. If the purchaser chooses to exercise this right, the seller must purchase the stock at the agreed strike price.

Put option Strike Price example

Let's stick to the same underlying as before and look at the strike price as it relates to the AAPL option.

Mr. A is buying a put in AAPL because he's expecting the price to come down in the next month or so. Since Mr. B is selling the put, let's assume that Mr. B thinks the price of the APPL is going to rise in the short term.

AAPL is currently trading at $145.52. Mr. A is looking to buy a put option at a price of (b) $140 and a debit of (c) $205. Mr. B sells it to Mr. A and gets a $205 credit.

From the case above (as the buyer of the put option), Mr. A hopes that the put option will expire in the money (i.e., when the stock price is less than the strike price).

Because Mr. B is selling the option to Mr. A, he's hoping that the option will expire out of the money (when the stock price is greater than the strike price) in order to retain the credit he got when they entered into the trade.

It is evident that the strike price is one of the key inputs to how much profit or loss a transaction can produce.

HOW TO HOOSE A STRIKE PRICE

Choosing a strike price is really not that difficult if you keep these things in mind:

Liquidity / Volume-one of the first things you want to consider when choosing a strike price is the liquidity of the underlying. If you choose a low-volume (i.e., not liquid) strike price, you may not be able to get filed on the trade or worse; you may not be able to exit the trade before it expires if the underlying is not liquid.

In the money versus Out of the money- is the option that you want to buy or sell in the money or out of the money? Based on the probabilities, in the money options are ideally suited to option buyers, and out of the money, options are ideally suited to option sellers.

Width of Strikes-when trading any strategy that involves spread (debit spread, credit spread, iron condor, and so on.), the width of the strike prices usually dictates the amount of risk you are ready to take, as well as the possibility of benefit. I.e., A five-point wide iron condor would hold significantly more risk than a one-point wide iron condor, but the possibility of profit and credit being received would be much higher.

Probability of in the money or Out of the money- Every strike price would have a different OTM or ITM probability. If you want to utilize the probabilities/statistics to determine what strike price to use, check the trade's probability of profit (POP).

SELLING COVERED CALLS

S elling covered calls is a method in which an investor writes a call option contract when at the same time, holding an equal number of shares of the underlying stock. Highly qualified market players write covered calls in order to boost investment income, but individual investors also can benefit from this conservative but efficient option strategy by taking out time to understand how and when to use it.

You are entitled to a variety of rights as owner of the stock or futures contract, which includes the right to sell the security at any given time for the market price. Covered call writing sells this right to somebody else in return for cash, ensuring that the option buyer has the right to own the protection on or before the expiry date at a fixed price called the strike price. A call option is a contract; it grants the purchaser the legal right (no obligation) to buy 100 shares of a futures contract or underlying stock at a strike price at any time on or prior to the date of expiration. If the owner of the call option also owns the underlying insurance, the option is called "covered" this is because he/she can deliver the instrument without buying it on the open market at probably unfavorable prices.

Selling a call obliges you to sell the stock you own already at the strike price A if the option is allocated.

Some investors run this strategy because they've already seen some good gains. They often sell out-of-the-money calls, so if the stock price rises, they 're willing to let go of the stock and take the profit.

Covered calls may also be used to generate income on the stock above and beyond a dividend. The goal, therefore, is to ensure that the options expire without worth.

If you buy the stock and sell the calls at the same time, it's called "Buy/Write." Some investors use Buy/Write as a method to decrease the cost base of the stock they've just bought.

Benefiting from Covered Calls

The purchaser pays the call option seller a premium in order to obtain the right to purchase contracts or shares at a preset future price. The premium is a cash charge paid on the day an option is sold, and it is the seller's money, whether or not the option is exercised. The covered call is thus, most lucrative if the stock moves up to the strike price, creating profit from the long stock position, while the call sold expires without worth, enabling the call writer to receive the full premium from its sale.

When you should sell a covered call

Whenever you sell a covered call, you get paid for giving up a portion of the future upside. Let's say, for example, that you buy ABC stock at $50 per share, assuming that it will grow to $60 in one year. You 're also able to sell $55 in six months, giving up more upside while getting a short-term profit. In this case, selling a covered call on the position may be an enticing strategy.

The stock options chain shows that offering a $55 six-month call option would cost the purchaser $4 per share premium. You may sell that option against your shares, which you bought at $50 and expect to sell at $60 in a year. Writing the covered call establishes an obligation to sell the stock at $55 in six months if the underlying price gets to that level. You'll get to retain the $4 premium plus $55 from the sale of the share, for a total sum of $59, or an 18% return in six months.

Meanwhile, if the stock drops to $40, you will suffer a $10 loss on the original position. However, you can keep the $4 premium from the sale of your call option, reducing the entire loss from $10 to $6 per share.

Benefits of Covered Calls

Selling covered call options can help to offset downside risks or add to upside returns, taking the cash premium for future upside beyond the strike price plus the premium during the contract period. In other words, if ABC's stock in the example closes beyond $59, the seller makes a lesser amount of money than if he/she simply held the stock. However, if the stock expires the six-month duration of less than $59 per share, the seller gains more money or loses a smaller amount of money than if the selling of options had not taken place.

Risks of covered calls

Call sellers must hold on to the underlying contracts or shares, or they will hold naked calls that have theoretically limitless potential for loss if the underlying security increases. Sellers, therefore, have to buy back options positions before they expire if they want to sell shares or contracts, increase transaction costs while decreasing net gains or increasing net losses.

Use covered calls to minimize the cost base or to earn income from shares or from futures contracts, to add a profit generator to the stock or to the ownership of the contract.

Like every other strategy, the covered call writing has pros and cons. When used together with the appropriate stock, covered calls can be an effective way to cut your average cost or to generate income.

Marketing:

This strategy is often advertised as 'conservative' or 'safe' and even 'hedging risk' as it offers premium income, but its shortcomings have been widely known since 1975 when Fischer Black released 'Fact and Fiction in the Use of Options.' According to Reilly and Brown, "To be profitable, the call strategy in question requires the investor to correctly assume that the share values will remain in a relatively narrow band around their current levels."

This form of option is best used when an investor needs to generate income from a long position when the market moves sideways. It enables an investor/writer to pursue a buy-and-hold strategy to make money out of a stock that is currently inactive in earnings. The investor/writer must properly conclude that the stock does not make any profits within the timeframe of the option; this is better achieved by writing out-of-the-money options. A covered call has a lower risk compared to other options types, which means that the potential reward is also lower.

MISTAKES TO BE AVOIDED WHEN SELLING COVERED CALLS

1: Sale for the wrong Strike Price or Expiration

If it comes to trading stocks, strategy is all that's needed. One of the major errors new investors make is opting to sell calls at a wrong strike price or expiration, without a good knowledge of the risks and rewards involved in any selling strategy.

The strike price is the price at which the call option will be exercised, and it has an immense effect on how profitable the investment can be. While choosing the correct strike price, you want to weigh your tolerance for risks as well as your ideal payoff.

For example, an out-of-the-money (OTM) call has a strike price, which is higher than the present stock price.

For instance, if an investor purchases 100 shares of the stock at $50 per share and sells a call option at a strike price of $ 50, they can collect a premium of $2 for every share ($200). If the buyer paid $5,000 to buy the stock and received $200 to write the call option, the entire cost per share will be $48 ($50-$2).

When the stock dropped to $48 a share, the option will expire without worth and still retain the $200 premium. However, if the stock rises past the purchase price of $ 50 at the time of expiration, the stock will be "called away" from the investor. You 're selling your shares at $50, and you're still keeping your $200 option premium.

The In-the-Money (ITM) option has a strike price lower than the prevailing market price. By selling an ITM option, you 're collecting more premiums, but also adding your chances of being called away.

When trading options, you also need to select an expiration date. Nowadays, it is common for several stocks to have options that would expire every week, month, quarter, and year.

While call sellers will receive a higher premium for an option with a longer date, the term of the contract is also longer. Due to time decay, call sellers derive the best benefit from shorter-term options.

2: Selling naked instead of covered

When it has to do with selling covered calls, a premium is the highest profit you can earn (in the example above, $200 was the premium and the highest possible payout).

If the underlying asset dramatically increases its price, the investor can face major losses if they do not own the shares. That's why most option writers do have a stake in the underlying asset, meaning that they own the stock also and are not only writing options on the stock they don't own.

Owning the stock on which you write an option is called writing a covered call. If you don't own the stock or the underlying security, it's referred to as writing a naked call.

A naked call strategy is naturally risky because there is minimal upside potential and almost infinite downside potential if the trade is against you.

Investors may even be forced to buy shares of the asset before expiration if the thresholds of the margin are not met. Based on the cost of the underlying stock, this may result in significant losses in earnings.

Due to the risk involved, new investors should concentrate on selling covered calls to stocks that they either already own or would not mind owning (and also have the capital to purchase).

3: Forget about the dividends

When it comes to determining option prices, you may just want to make sure that you take dividends into account before choosing the right stock.

If you bought 100 shares, you would obtain dividend payments if the ex-date is between the time of purchase and the expiration date, in addition to any premium you may receive from selling a call.

Dividend payments before expiration will have an impact on the call premium. Because the stock price is anticipated to fall by the dividend payment on the ex-dividend date, the call premiums will become lower, and the premiums will become higher. Dividend payments are also a common reason for call buyers to exercise their options early. According to The Motley Fool, the reinvested dividends account for 42% of the large-cap stock returns, 36% of the middle cap returns, and 31% of the small-cap returns. Dividends paying stocks often outperform their non-paying equivalents year on year.

That's why it's important to take stock dividends into account when selecting the underlying security for your options trade. You can also choose to reinvest your dividends later if more capital is needed.

4: Not having a loss management plan

Another common error that new investors make is that they don't prepare for a trade to move against them.

While no one desires for a trade to go bad, it is important that you still prepare for a loss and managing risk. This means deciding how much money you 're willing to lose before you trade, and how you're going to bail out a trade if it turns sour, so you fully know when you're going to cut your losses.

You should create a plan for what a reasonable profit goal would be, based on the historical activities of the underlying asset, with sufficient space for flexibility just in case the economy becomes unstable and stock prices rise or fall sharply.

Bear in mind there's no one-size-fits-all approach to cutting the losses. Your risk management approach will primarily rely on your style of trading, account size, as well as position size.

The good news is that trading options will give you more flexibility when stock markets fall. For example, you always have the option to purchase back the call and eliminate the obligation to deliver the stock.

Just know, if the trade starts going against you, your first reaction shouldn't be to throw money at it. You should stick to your plan as much as you can (even if it's an exit plan), accept some loss if possible. Handling your emotions is a vital part of becoming a good investor. Not all trade will yield profit, but you can mitigate the risk by getting a good strategy before you begin investing.

5: Expecting Immediate Return

Eventually, options traders should be ready to invest for a long time and not expect returns immediately. While options trading can be lucrative, nothing is assured and in no way forms or shapes a "get rich fast" scheme.

It's still going to require some time to get the returns

you expect. A realistic target will be to bring about a return on your investment of about 10-12% per year.

Again, it is also important to have a plan if the returns are lower than expected, but most of the time, your method should be for consistent returns over some years, not months.

The Three Outcomes of Covered Calls

1. THE STOCK GOES DOWN

If the stock price is lower at the time of expiration of the option, the good news is that the call will expire without worth, and you will keep the full premium obtained for selling it. Apparently, the bad news is the value of the stock is low. That's the nature of the call. The risk emerges from the ownership of the stock. However, profit from selling the call can help to offset some of the losses on the stock.

If the stock drops before the call expires, do not panic. You're not stuck in your place. Because losses will accrue on the stock, the call option that was sold will also fall in value. That's a good thing because it's going to be possible to buy back a call for less money than you paid to sell it.

If your perspective on the stock changes, you can simply close your spot by repurchasing the call contract and dumping the stock.

2. THE STOCK STAYS THE SAME OR IT GOES UP A LITTLE, or IT DOES NOT GET TO THE STRIKE PRICE

In this case, there's no bad news. The call choice you've sold expires worthless, and you're going to pocket the whole premium from selling it. You may see some benefits on the underlying stock, which will still be yours.

3. THE STOCK RISES BEYOND THE STRIKE PRICE

If the stock is greater than the strike price rate at the expiration, the call option will be assigned, and you will be required to sell 100 shares of the stock.

When the stock is skyrocketing after you sell the shares, you don't have to kick yourself for losing out on any potential earnings. You made a deliberate decision that you were ready to sell the stock at the strike price, and that you have reached the full profit potential from the strategy.

Strategies for Buying Call

Buying Call Options

Remember that the call option grants an investor the right to purchase the underlying asset at a date in the future for the price specified today. Let's assume that you're looking at a stock that sells $31 per share, and you believe that the price will rise to $40 a share in the next few months. You observe that there's a call option on the stock with a strike price of $35 that expires in 5 months and is selling for $0.50 per option share. This implies that it will cost you $50 to invest in a single call contract since the standard option contracts are meant for 100 shares. If you're correct and the stock price rises to $40 per share before your option expires, you will be able to sell your option at least for its intrinsic value, i.e., the difference between the stock market price and the market price of the option, which is $5 per option share in this case. The profit on this particular transaction is $450 i.e., $500-$50 = $450. However, if you're wrong, and the stock price does not even rise to a $35 share, you 're going to lose your entire $50 investment. However, you should note that the option premium will always be substantially lower than the underlying stock price itself so that you can place a bet on a high-priced stock with significantly less money than would be needed to invest in the actual stock.

You could also make use of a call option to limit your exposure to risk in a short sale. A short sale means selling a stock that you do not own. You have to borrow the stock, via your broker, from the portfolio of another investor and sell it with an expectation that its price will go down, at which point you buy it back and then return it, making profits from the difference between the price you sold the stock short and the lower price with which you are able to buy it back. Of course, if the stock price does not fall as expected and instead keeps rising, theoretically, your losses could be unlimited. Meanwhile, if you buy a call option on the same stock at the same time as you make a short sale, you would have locked in the price at which you will buy the stock in the future in case the price goes up.

When you purchase a call, you pay the option premium as an exchange for the right to purchase shares at a fixed price (i.e., the strike price) on or before a certain date (the expiration date). Investors are more likely to purchase calls when they're bullish on a stock or other security because it provides leverage.

For instance, assume that ABC is trading for $50. The one-month call option for the stock costs $3. Would you prefer to buy 100 ABC shares for $5,000, or would you prefer to buy a single call option for $300 ($3 x 100 shares), with the payoff being dependent on the closing price of the stock one month from now?

Basics of call options

The purchaser of the call options has the right, not the obligation, to buy the underlying security at the stated strike price. This simply means that if you were to buy call options on ABC stock, for instance, you would have the right to purchase ABC stock at an agreed price before a certain date.

The main reason you may decide to purchase a call option, as opposed to merely buying a stock, is that options allow you to control the very same amount of stock with a lesser amount of money.

For example, if you had $5,000, you can buy 100

shares of a stock trading at $50 per share (with the exception of trading costs), or you can purchase call options that give you the right to purchase the same amount of shares for considerably less.

Characteristics of the call option

Compared to buying stock, buying a call option requires just a little more work. Knowing how options work is key to knowing whether buying calls is an effective strategy for you. There are several decisions that would have to be made before purchasing options. These include the following:

The security on which to purchase call options. Peradventure you think the stock of ABC Company would rise over a particular period of time, you may consider purchasing ABC call options.

The amount of trade that can be supported. This is the highest amount of money you would want to use to purchase your call options.

The number of options contracts to be purchased. Every options contract controls 100 shares of an underlying stock. For example, buying three call option contracts gives the right to the owner, but not the obligation, to purchase 300 shares (3 x 100 = 300).

The price of the strike/Strike Price.

The price at which the owner of the options may purchase the underlying security when the option is exercised is the strike price. For example, the ABC 50 call options give the owner the right to purchase ABC stock at $50, despite the current price of the market. In this case, $50 is the strike price (also known as the exercise price).

The amount to pay for the options. So although you buy the stock at the stock price, options are being bought for what is known as the premium. This is the amount it's going to cost to purchase options. For example, using the 50 ABC call options, the premium can be $3 per contract. Thus, the total cost of purchasing one ABC 50 call option contract will be $300 ($3 premium per contract x 100 shares controlled by the options x 1 total contract = $300). If the premium was $4 per contract, instead of $3, the overall cost of purchasing three contracts would be $1,200 ($4 per contract x 100 shares controlled by the options x 3 overall contracts = $1,200).

The month of expiration. Options do not last for an indefinite period; they have an expiration date. If the stock closes below the strike price and the call option has not been exercised by the date of expiration, it expires without worth, and the purchaser no longer has right to purchase the underlying asset and also loses the premium he or she has paid for the option. Most stocks have option contracts that usually last up to nine months. Traditional options contracts usually expire on the third Friday of every month.

The type of order. Just like stocks, the prices of options change constantly. As a result, you can decide the trading order to purchase an options contract with. There are different types of orders, which include market, limit, stop-loss, stop-limit, trailing-stop-loss, and trailing-stop-limit.

Time value of money (TVM)

The idea that money currently available is worth more than the exact amount in the future due to its potential earning capacity is the time value of money. The central concept of finance is that as long as money can generate interest, every sum of money is worth more the faster it is earned. One of the most basic concepts in finance is that money has a time value connected to it. In other words, the dollar was worth more yesterday than it is today, and tomorrow the dollar is worth more than the dollar. The idea that money you currently have is worth more than the same amount in the future because of its prospective earning capacity is the time value of money. The central concept of finance is that the money given will generate interest; every sum of money is worth more the faster it is earned. TVM is referred to sometimes as the present discounted value. The time value of money is gotten from the idea that rational investors would rather receive money today rather than the exact amount of money in the future because of the potential of money to increase in value over a given time period. For example, money invested in a savings account generates a certain interest rate and is thus said to increase its value.

There are five (5) variables you have to know about:

Present Value (PV)-This is your present starting value. It's the money you've got in your hand at the moment, your initial investment for the future.

Future Value (FV)-This is the final amount at some

point in the future. It should be worth much more than the present value, given that interest is earned and grows over time.

The number of periods (N)-This has to do with the timeline for your investment (or debt). It is typically measured in years, but it could also be any time scale, such as quarterly, monthly, and even daily.

Interest rate (I)- This is your money's growth rate over the lifespan of the investment. It is expressed as a percentage value, such as 8% or .08.

Payment amount (PMT)- They are a series of equivalent, evenly spaced cash flows.

It's possible to calculate the fifth variable if you have four of the five variables listed above. A representative example of this would be: if you spend one dollar (PV) for a year (N) at 6% (I), you will get $1.06 (FV). It will be the same as saying that the present value of $1.06 that you expect to get in one year is just $1.00 (PV).

The formula for calculating Time Value of Money

The time value of money is a vital concept not only for people but also for business decision - making.

Organizations weigh the time value of money when making decisions regarding investing in new product growth, getting new business facilities and equipment, and setting credit terms for the sales of their products and services.

For the estimation of the future value of income, a particular formula can be used so that it can be related to the present value:

The formula for Time Value of Money

$FV = PV \times (1+i)n$

Where:

FV is the future value

PV is the present value (the original amount of money)

I is the Interest rate for each time.

n is the number of periods

Suppose that Catherine is putting \$100 in the bank for 5 years at 5% interest, and fit that into the equation.

$FV = 100 \ (+0.05)5$

$FV = 100 \ x \ 1.2762$

FV = $127.62

Present Value

Catherine's parents think she's a very smart girl, especially after showing her dad these awesome formulas. Dad knows he's going to need money in a couple of years to pay for Catherine's college. He 's thinking how much he should invest in some CDs that will be worth $20,000 or thereabout in 10 years when he's going to need it. Catherine shows him the formula for calculating present value, or how much is needed to save now to have a certain amount at some time in the future. Here is the formula:

$$PV = FV/1 + r)$$

where,

PV is how much that's needed to have today/present value.

R is the interest rate he's going to earn

N is the number of periods until the money is required, and

FV is how much he will require in the future/future

value.

So, if Dad needs $20,000 in 10 years and can invest what he's got for 5%, let 's see how much he needs to invest now.

PV = $20,000/(1.05)10

PV = $20,000/1,6289;

PV = $12,278

Volatility

Volatility is a measure based on statics of the distribution of returns for a particular market or security index. In most case, the higher the volatility, the more risky the security. Volatility is usually measured either as the standard deviation or the variance between the returns from that same security or market index.

Volatility in financial markets is often correlated with broad swings in either direction. For instance, when the stock market goes up and down more than 1% for a prolonged period of time, it is considered a "volatile" market. The volatility of an asset is a crucial factor when it comes to pricing options contracts.

Volatility is also the amount of uncertainty or risk associated with the size of the change in the value of the security. Higher volatility implies that the value of the security will potentially be distributed over a broad range of values. It implies that the price of the security may change drastically in any direction within a short period of time. Lower volatility implies that the value of the security does not fluctuate drastically and appears to be more stable.

One way to calculate the change in the asset is to quantify the daily returns (% transfer on a daily basis) of the asset. Historical volatility is founded on historical prices and reflects the degree of uncertainty in asset returns. This number has no unit, and it is expressed in percentage. Although variance captures the distribution of returns around the mean asset in general, volatility is the measure of that variance bound by a particular period of time. Thus, we can monitor daily, weekly, monthly, or annual volatility. It is, therefore, useful to view volatility as an annual standard deviation, i.e., volatility = $\sqrt{\text{variance}}$ annualized

How to calculate the volatility

Volatility is usually calculated, employing variance and standard deviations. Standard deviation is the square root of variance.

For convenience, let 's say that we have a monthly stock price of $1 through $10. For instance, the first month is $1; the second month is $2, and so on. Here are the five steps below to calculate variance.

Calculate the mean for the data set. This implies adding each value and dividing it by the total number of values. If $1, $2, $3, all through to $10 are added together, we'll get $55. It is then divided by 10, as we've got ten numbers in the data collection. This provides a mean or an average price of $5.50.

Calculate the difference between the value of each data and the mean. This is often referred to as a deviation. For instance, we'll take $10-$5.50 = $4.50, then $9-$5.50 = $3.50. This goes all the way down to our first $1 data value. Negative numbers are permissible. Because we need each value, such calculations are always performed in a spreadsheet.

Square the deviations. It is going to remove negative

values.

Add up the squared deviations together. This is equal to 82.5 in the example.

Divide the sum of the squared deviation, i.e., 82.5 by the number of data values.

The resulting variance, in this case, is $8.25. The square root is used to calculate the standard deviation. This will give $2.87. It is a measure of risk that demonstrates how prices are distributed all around the average price. It gives traders an insight into how much the price could deviate from the average.

If prices are sampled randomly from a normal distribution, about 68% of all data values will fall within one standard deviation. 95% of the data will fall within two standard deviations (2 x 2.87 according to the example), and 99.7% of all the values will come within three standard deviations (S.D.), i.e., 3 x 2.87. In such case, the values of $1 to $10 are not distributed randomly on a bell curve. They are evenly distributed. As a result, the predicted 68% − 95% − 99.7% do not hold. Despite the limitation, standard deviations are still widely used by traders, as price returns data sets frequently represent a regular (bell curve) distribution more than in the example given.

Other Measures of Volatility

Beta (β) is the measure of the relative volatility of a particular stock on the market. The beta approximates the total volatility of the security returns against the returns of an appropriate benchmark (generally, the S&P 500 is utilized). For instance, a stock that has a beta value of 1.1 hashat moved historically at a price level of 110% for each 100%. Alternatively, the stock with a beta of .9 has traditionally shifted 90% of every 100% in the underlying index.

Market volatility can also be seen in the Volatility Index or VIX. VIX was set up by the Chicago Board of Options Exchange as a means to measure the 30-day volatility expected of the U.S. stock market resulting from the S&P 500 call and put options in real-time quotes prices. This is essentially a measure of future bets made by investors and traders on the direction of the market or on individual securities. High reading on the VIX signifies a risky market.

Volatility, which is expressed as a percentage coefficient within the option-pricing formulae, arises from daily trading activities. The value of the coefficient used would be influenced by how the volatility is measured.

Volatility is also used for pricing options contracts using models such as Black-Scholes or binomial tree models. More volatile underlying assets will result in higher options premiums because, with uncertainty, there is a greater likelihood that options will eventually wind up in-the-money at expiration. Option traders attempt to forecast the future volatility of the asset, and therefore the market option price reflects its implied volatility.

Stock Rights

Stock rights refer to the privilege given to existing shareholders to gain extra common stock shares when a new issue is placed on the marketplace. Generally, the stock right enables the shareholder to receive additional shares in the exact proportion as their shares which are already existing.

A stock warrant is a document detailing the rights

given to stockholders, including the number of shares that may be bought as well as the purchase price.

Companies may issue extra common stock shares in the market in order to generate capital. A rights issue gives existing shareholders an opportunity to retain their proportional ownership of a company by permitting them to gain extra shares of a new share issue in the exact proportion as their existing shares. For example, if the new issue of shares increases the number of shares outstanding by 10%, the shareholder holding 100 shares will have the right to buy ten shares of the new issue.

The information provided on the warrant includes the number of shares that can be bought, the price per share, and the date on which the right expires. Warrants are long-term tools that also enables shareholders to buy extra shares at a discounted price, but are typically issued at an exercise price beyond the current market price. As a result, a waiting period of probably six months to a year is allocated to the warrants, which provides the stock price time to increase enough to surpass the exercise price and to provide intrinsic value. Warrants are typically sold in combination with set income securities and serve as a "sweetener" or financial incentive to buy a bond or preferred stock.

A single warrant can typically buy a single share of the stock, even though it is designed to buy more or less than that in some instances. Warrants have also been used rarely to buy other types of securities, like favored offerings or bonds. Warrants differ from rights in that they have to be bought from a broker for commission and generally qualify as marginal securities.

In some respects, both rights and warrants are conceptually similar to publicly traded call options. The value of the three instruments is inherently dependent on the price of the underlying stock. They also look like market options in that they do not have voting rights and don't pay dividends or offer any kind of claim to the company.

The investor has three options when the stock rights are granted:

Purchase Shares: the shareholder may elect to exercise his right to purchase additional shares of stock.

Sell rights: if the warrant price is less than the current

market price for one share, the stock rights have value. If this happens, the shareholder may sell stock rights to another investor to earn a profit.

Do Nothing: eventually, the shareholder may permit the rights to be expired without buying extra shares or selling the rights.

Once the rights issue has been announced, the share cannot be separated from the rights, and the new shares are referred to as rights-on. As soon as the warrant has been issued, both the shares and the rights can be separately sold. When a share of the stock is separately sold from its rights, it is referred to as ex-rights.

RIGHT AND WARRANTS VERSUS OPTIONS

R ights and warrants vary from market options in that they are issued initially only to current shareholders. However, a secondary market usually exists that enables other buyers to purchase these securities.

Shareholders who obtain rights and warrants possess four options at their disposal:

Keep their rights or warrants for the meantime.

Purchase extra rights or warrants from the secondary market

Sell their rights or warrants to some other investor.

Simply allow the expiration of their rights or warrants.

The final method mentioned here is not the best one to be adopted by investors. If the present market price of the stock is more than the exercise price, investors who do not wish to exercise it should always sell it on the secondary market in order to gain its own intrinsic value.

However, many uninformed stockholders who lack an understanding of the value of their rights do this regularly.

Value Determination

As with market options, the market price of the stock could fall below the exercise price, in which case the rights or warrants will become worthless. Rights and warrants become worthless on expiration, regardless of whether the underlying stock is being traded. Stock rights and warrant values are determined in very much the same way as market options. They have both an intrinsic value, which is equivalent to the difference between both the market and the exercise stock prices, and a time value, which is founded on the stock's potential to increase in price before the expiry date.

Both types of securities, irrespective of the present price of the underlying stock, will become worthless when expired. They will also end up losing their intrinsic value if the market price of the shares drops below their exercise or subscription price. For this reason, companies must carefully set exercise prices on these issues in order to minimize the chance that the whole offer will fail.

However, rights and warrants may also give shareholders substantial gains in the same way as to call options if the underlying stock price increases.

OPTIONS BUYING

Put Options

Buying a put option offers you the right to sell a stock at a particular price – the strike price – at any time before a certain date. This means that anyone who sold you the option– the writer – can be asked to pay the strike price to you for the stock at any point before the expiration of the time. Nevertheless, you are not under any obligation to do that.

Purchasing put options is a method to hedge against a potential fall in share prices. They could also reap profits from bear markets or decrease the prices of individual stocks.

Risk of put options

Options are derivatives, which means that they get their value from the underlying security. Trading in derivatives can be far more complex and risky than trading stocks and bonds.

Based on the type of derivative, losses can be more

than the amount invested. In the worst-case situation, losses for certain derivatives can be almost infinite.

Hedging with Put Options

One use for put options is to hedge against a possible fall in the share prices of your portfolio. Assuming you own 100 shares of a stock priced at $100 per share. You are worried that the stock may fall to $90 in the next three months.

You may purchase a put option that gives you the right to sell 100 shares of the stock at a strike price of $ 100 at any point in the next three months. Because you own the shares, this is referred to as a covered trade.

Option prices vary, but let's assume this one costs $2 per share. This is $200 for a regular lot of 100 shares.

If the stock drops to $90 or less during that time, you may ask the writer to buy each of your shares for $100. It would keep you from losing more than the $200 cost of the option.

If the three-month period passes without shares becoming less than $100, you will allow the option to expire without exercising it. You would have expended

$200 without getting anything but your peace of mind.

Buying Uncovered Put Options

You can also purchase put options for shares that you don't own. But before you exercise the uncovered put option, you have to purchase the shares.

You can buy put options as well as individual securities. This can result in profits from large declines in bear markets.

If the price of the option shares in the previous example had dropped to $90, the purchaser of the uncovered put option could still have asked the writer to buy 100 shares for $100 each. First of all, he or she would buy up the shares for $90 each. After paying a $200 option premium, this put option would gain $800.

The prices of the shares may not fall below the strike price. The put option buyer would then allow the option to expire unused. The $200 would've been spent for no profit.

Purchasing uncovered put options grants an investor a lot of leverage. In this example, the investor manages $10,000 worth of shares at the cost of only $200. The

$200 is all that the investor risks.

However, the potential profit in this instance is as high as $10,000, or $9,800, after the $200 option premium, if the value of the share drops to zero.

How to Buy Options

You need to open an account with an options broker to purchase put options. The broker will then assign a level of trading to you. It restricts the type of trade you can trade on the basis of your experience, financial capital, and risk tolerance.

To buy a put option, firstly pick a strike price. It would usually be far below where the stock is currently being traded.

Next, pick a date of expiration. Usually, that may be from one month to one year in the future. Longer periods generally mean fewer risks.

Next, determine how many contracts you need to purchase. Each option contract is for 100 shares of the stock. For each contract, you will pay the premium listed for that option, including brokerage fees.

After you pay, watch the stock prices to see if it's time

to exercise the option. You can decide to exercise this option at any time before the expiry date.

If current prices drop below the strike price, the option is taken to be in the money. You may need the option writer to buy your shares at a higher strike price if your option is in the money.

If the stock price does not fall, you can allow the option to expire. You 're not going to make anything, but your losses will be restricted to the cost of options and fees.

SELLING A PUT

S elling/writing a put option enables an investor to actually own the underlying security at a later date in the future and at a much more appropriate price. In other words, selling a put option allows market players to acquire bullish exposure, with the additional benefit of potentially possessing the underlying security at a date in the future and at a price less than the current market price.

Call Options vs. Put Options

A fast primer on options can be helpful to enable you to understand how writing/selling puts will boost your investment strategies.

An equity option is a derivative tool that derives its value from the underlying assets. Buying a call option grants the holder the right to own the security at a set price, known as the exercise price option. Alternatively, the option provided gives the owner the right to sell the underlying security at an option exercise price. So, buying a call option is a bullish bet- the owner earns a profit when the security goes up-while the put option is a bearish bet- the owner earns a profit when the security goes down.

Selling a call or put option overturns this directional logic. More importantly, the writer assumes an obligation to the counterparty while selling the option, and he has a duty to uphold the position of the purchaser of the option wants to exercise his right to own the security.

Here's a rundown of the choices for buying versus selling.

Buying a call-You have the right to purchase a security at a set price.

Selling a call- You have a duty to provide security at a fixed price to an option buyer if they exercise that option.

Buying a Put-You have the right to sell the security at a fixed price.

Selling a Put- You have an obligation to purchase the security at a predetermined price from the option buyer if the option has been exercised.

Characteristics of Prudently selling Put

Sell puts only when you are comfortable owning the underlying security at a fixed price because you assume an obligation to purchase if the other person decides to exercise the option.

Enter trades only where the net price paid for the underlying security is appealing. This is the most important consideration when selling puts profitably in a market environment. (There are other reasons to sell, particularly when implementing more complicated options strategies.)

Other benefits of selling put may be exploited once this major pricing rule has been satisfied. The ability to generate portfolio income is at the top of this list, as the seller gets to keep the whole premium if the amount sold expires without being exercised by the other person.

Another main advantage is the chance of owning the underlying security at a price less than the current market price.

CONCLUSION

OPTIONS STRATEGIES

1. Covered call

With calls, one of the strategies is basically to purchase a naked call option. You can also set up a basic, covered call or buy-write. This is a very common strategy as it produces income and eliminates some risk of being long the stock on its own. The trade-off is this; you have to be ready to sell your shares at a fixed price-a short strike price. To implement this strategy, you buy the underlying stock as you would normally, and at the same time write/or sell a call option on the same shares.

In this example, we use the call option on the stock, which represents 100 shares of the stock per call option. Around the same time, you sell one call option on every 100 shares of the stock you buy. It is known as a covered call because, in the event that a stock rocket is of a higher price, the short call is covered by a long stock position. Investors may use this strategy if they have a short-term stock position and a neutral stance on their direction. They may try to generate income (through selling the call premium) or to protect against a possible decrease in the value of the underlying stock.

2. Married Put

In the married put strategy, an investor buys an asset (in this case, shares of the stock) and, at the same time, buys put options for an equal number of shares. The options holder has the right to sell the stock at the strike price. Each contract has a worth of 100 shares. The reason that an investor would utilize this strategy is primarily to protect their potential risk when holding a stock. This strategy functions much like an insurance policy and sets a price floor in case the stock price falls sharply.

An illustration of a married put would be when an investor purchases 100 shares of the stock and buys one option at the same time. This strategy is enticing because an investor is safeguarded to the downside if a negative event occurs. At the same time, the buyer would have shared in all of the gains if the stock had risen in value. The only problem with this strategy is if the stock doesn't drop, in which case the investor then loses the premium paid for the put option.

3. Bull Call Spread

In this strategy, an investor will simultaneously purchase calls at a particular strike price and sell the exact number of calls at a higher strike price. Both call options would have the same expiry date and underlying asset. This type of vertical spread strategy is mostly used when an investor is bullish and expects a moderate increase in the price of the asset. The investor limits his / her business upside but decreases the net premium he/she spends by purchasing a naked call option.

4. Bear Put Spread

This strategy is also a type of vertical spread. In this strategy, the investor simultaneously purchases options at a particular strike price and sell the same amount of puts at a lower strike price. Both options will be for the same underlying asset and also have the same expiry date. This strategy is utilized when the investor is bearish and predicts the price of the underlying asset to decrease. It gives limited losses and limited gains.

5. Protective Collar

A protective collar strategy is implemented by purchasing an out-of-the-money put option and also writing an out-of-the-money call option at a corresponding time for the same underlying asset and its expiration. This strategy is often adopted by investors after substantial gains have been made in a long position in the stock. This combination of options allows investors to have downside security while potentially obliging them to sell shares at a higher price, i.e., selling higher = more income than at current stock levels.

A simple example would be if the investor had a long 100 shares of Motorola at $50, and Motorola had increased to $100 as of 1st of January. The investor may create a protective collar by selling one Motorola 15th of March 105 call and simultaneously buying one Motorola March 95 put. The trader is secured below $95 till the 15th of March, with the trade-off potentially having an obligation to sell his shares at $105.

6. Long straddle

This strategy is when an investor simultaneously buys a put option and a call option on an underlying asset, at the same strike price and an expiry date. An investor will often utilize this strategy when he/she believes that the price of the underlying asset will significantly move out of range, but is uncertain in which direction the move will take. This approach allows the investor to have the chance for virtually unlimited gains, whereas the maximum loss is limited to the combined costs of both options contracts.

7. Long Strangle

In this strategy, an investor buys an out-of-the-money call option as well as an out-of-the-money put option at the same on the same underlying asset and expiry date. An investor who uses this strategy is of the opinion that the price of the underlying asset will experience a really large movement, but is unsure in which direction the movement will be.

This could be, for instance, a wager on the release of earnings for a company or probably an FDA event for stock in healthcare. Losses are restricted to the cost (or the premium spent) of both options. Strangles will often always be cheaper than straddles because the options bought are out of the money.

8. Long Call Butterfly Spread

Up to this level, all the strategies mentioned are a combination of two separate contracts or positions. In a long butterfly spread making use of call options, an investor combines a bull spread strategy and the bear spread strategy, using three distinct strike prices. Both options are for the same underlying asset and expiry date.

For instance, a long butterfly spread can be made by buying one in-the-money call option at a lesser strike price while selling two in-the-money call options and purchasing one out-of-the-money call option. A balanced butterfly spread has the same wing width. This example is referred to as a call fly and leads to a net debit. Investors would enter a long butterfly call spread when they feel the stock is not going to move much by expiration.

9. Iron Condor

The iron condor is an even more intriguing strategy. In this strategy, the investor holds a bull spread and a bear call spread at the same time. The Iron Condor is formed by selling one out-of-the-money put and purchasing one out-of-money put off a much lower strike (bull put spread) and selling one out-of-the-money call and buying one out-of-money call for a higher strike (bear call spread). All options have the same date of expiration and are all on a similar underlying asset. Typically, the put and call sides have the same width of spread. This trading strategy earns a net structural premium and is constructed to take advantage of the low-volatility stock. Many traders like this trade because of their presumed high probability of receiving a small amount of premium.

10. Iron Butterfly

In this strategy, an investor sells an in-the-money put and purchases an out-of-the-money put. He also sells an in-the-money call and buys an out-of-the-money call. All options have the same date of expiration and are on the same underlying asset. Though it is similar to a butterfly spread, this strategy is different because it uses both puts and calls, as opposed to one or the other.

In essence, this strategy combines selling an in-the-money straddle and buying protective wings. You can also assume the construction to be two spreads. It is common for both spreads to have the same width. The long, out-of-the-money call secures against limitless downsides. The long out-of-the-money put protects against the downside from a short put strike to zero. Profit and loss are limited within a particular range and is dependent on the strike price of the options used. Investors prefer this strategy because it generates higher income, and there is a higher probability of a little gain with a stock that is non-volatile.

Do Not Go Yet; One Last Thing To Do

If you enjoyed this book or found it useful, I'd be very grateful if you'd post a short review on Amazon. Your support does make a difference, and I read all the reviews personally so I can get your feedback and make this book even better.

Thanks for your help and support!